D0192818

Managing
Your
Career

The Lessons Learned Series

Through the power of personal storytelling, each book in
the Lessons Learned series presents the accumulated wisdom of some of the world's best known experts, and offers insights into how these individuals think, how they
approach new challenges, and how they use hard-won lessons from experience to shape their leadership philosophies. Organized thematically, according to the topics at
the top of managers' agendas, each book draws from Fifty
Lessons' extensive video library of interviews with CEOs
and other thought leaders. Here, the world's leading senior executives, academics, and business thinkers speak directly and candidly about their triumphs and defeats.
Taken together, these powerful stories offer the advice
you'll need to take on tomorrow's challenges.

Other books in the series:

Leading by Example
Managing Change

⊰ LESSONS LEARNED ⊱

Managing Your Career

Harvard Business School Press
Boston, Massachusetts

Printed in the United States of America
11 10 09 08 07   5 4 3 2 1

Library of Congress Cataloging-in-Publication Data
Managing your career.
    p. cm. — (Lessons learned)
  ISBN-13: 978-1-4221-1861-0 (pbk. : alk. paper)
  1. Career development. 2. Vocational guidance. I.
Harvard Business School Publishing Corporation.
  HF5381.M2864 2007
  650.14—dc22

                                        2007019475

⊰ A NOTE FROM THE ⊱
PUBLISHER

In partnership with Fifty Lessons, a leading provider of digital media content, Harvard Business School Press is pleased to announce the launch of Lessons Learned, a new book series that showcases the trusted voices of the world's most experienced leaders. Through the power of personal storytelling, each book in this series presents the accumulated wisdom of some of the world's best-known experts and offers insights into how these individuals think, approach new challenges, and use hard-won lessons from experience to shape their leadership philosophies. Organized thematically according to the topics at the top of managers' agendas—leadership, change management, entrepreneurship, innovation, and strategy, to name a few—each book draws from Fifty Lessons' extensive video library of interviews with CEOs and other thought leaders.

A Note from the Publisher

Here, the world's leading senior executives, academics, and business thinkers speak directly and candidly about their triumphs and defeats. Taken together, these powerful stories offer the advice you'll need to take on tomorrow's challenges.

We invite you to join the conversation now. You'll find both new ways of looking at the world, and the tried-and-true advice you need to illuminate the path forward.

⊰ CONTENTS ⊱

Contents

Managing
Your
Career

Choose Your Words Carefully

Paul Anderson

Chairman, Spectra Energy

AS I PROGRESSED in my career and got into increasingly more responsible or powerful roles, I had to be more sensitive to the impact that my words had on individuals and organizations.

It was almost like my words took on the power of the position, and things that were casual before were no longer casual. I had

my first example of this when I was a manager. It was fairly early in my career, and a
young woman named Sarah had come in. I
was running a planning organization, and
Sarah came to me and said, "Look, I don't
have any background in planning—I'm from
the IT group—but I would love to join your
organization. I'll work hard to learn what I
need to learn to do a good job. I will strive
to do anything that you need done. Just give
me a chance."

I said, "Well that sounds fair to me. Why
don't you join the organization? I'll give
you a year. And at the end of a year you will
either be a planner and contributing; or, if
it's not working out, you can go back to the
IT group, and we'll just assume that it was a
nice try but it didn't work out."

So she joined the organization and she
was outstanding; she was the best new employee we had that year. She took on everything; she learned. She became the "go-to'"
person—everybody came to her with their
issues. She was a star, there was just no question; she was doing an outstanding job.

And I thought, "Well, this has to be one of the best moves that I've ever participated in," and I was quite comfortable that things were working out nicely. But at the end of a year, she came into my office, and she was in tears. I said, "Sarah, what's wrong?" And she said, "Well, I don't understand why it's not working out. At the end of a year, you said you'd tell me if it was working out and you haven't told me that, so I must assume that it's not working out and I'm going to have to go back to IT." I was flabbergasted, and of course I told her, "Hey, you're doing a great job!"

But it struck me that I had made a casual comment: ". . . in a year we'll know." She had gone back to her office and marked her calendar, and, by God, at the end of a year she expected me to walk into her office with a decision. That casual comment had been so powerful to her, and so insignificant to me, that it really struck me that I had to be very careful in making comments as I went along.

As I got higher in the organization, it just got worse. The organization would hang on words, they'd look for hidden meanings, they would dissect casual comments; and I found by the time I was CEO of a company that there is no such thing as "off the record." Anything you say, once it's said, becomes indelibly imprinted in people's minds, and they pay attention to it. So I would make a comment, and people would dissect it—they would say, "What does this mean? Is there a hidden meaning here?"

Often I would appear on the front page of a paper or in an analyst report, and a careless comment could actually move the stock price or upset an employee base. When I was at BHP Billiton, if I made a casual comment about availability of copper or production of copper or something like that, London's metal market would actually move.

So I learned that you really have to watch what you're saying as you get higher in the organization, because your voice carries so much more weight than you yourself believe it does.

The other thing I learned along those lines is that you really have to watch and be very careful about your use of humor and hyperbole, because what you think might be a cute comment might be taken very literally. You want to avoid hyperbole that says, "We're going to knock them dead"—somebody might actually go out there and do something about that! So you really have to be cautious as to what you say.

If I look back on what I've learned here in terms of the impact that your words have, [I'd have to say] that once you reach a position of power, whatever it is, and people are starting to pay attention to you, you need to be very sensitive and think it through: "If I were the listener taking everything that I heard absolutely literally, what would I be hearing?"

You almost need to say the words without emotion in your mind—because you're coloring it in your own mind as to whether it's humorous or casual or totally off the record—and just look at it as if it were a statement that could be on the front page of the paper tomorrow. You have to say, "If it were on the front page of the paper, one, would I be embarrassed, and two, would I regret that I'd ever said it?"

TAKEAWAYS

- As you progress in your career, you must watch what you're saying: your voice carries so much more weight to those around you than you might imagine.

- You should assume that every comment you make will be noted and analyzed, both in the press and internally. There is no such thing as "off the record" when you are management within an organization.

- You might practice being more sensitive about what you say to colleagues in passing; consider why you are in dialogue with them and consider what will be important to them.

Smart Managers Don't Repeat Mistakes

Sir Richard Evans

Chairman, United Utilities

THERE WAS A VERY FAMOUS GUY called "T." Wilson, who really was the éminence grise of the Boeing airplane company for many years. In fact, he was the guy who, in the postwar period, built up the Boeing airplane company.

Managing Your Career

When I got to know T. Wilson—he was a lot older than I was—I was lucky enough one day to be having a drink with him. He was the guy who brought the Boeing 707 to the marketplace, which was really the first highly successful commercial jet airplane. Like a lot of other things, the Brits got there first but simply never turned it into a serious business venture. These guys in Boeing did it. But as a result, the demand for the aircraft rose so quickly that they were buying immense volumes of aluminum, which was a major piece of the material for the construction of the aircraft.

I was asking him, when he looked back over his career, what were the most difficult times he'd had in dealing with the investment communities and the analysts of the New York markets. He reminded me of a situation that I'd heard about briefly but didn't really understand. They were buying such big volumes of aluminum at the time, and the lead time on taking an order and delivering an aircraft was three to four years—depending on the market supply and demand—so prices fluctuated violently. It's very similar to the oil situation today, actually. So you could sell an aircraft and assume a price for aluminum of X dollars per kilo, but by the time you actually came to buy it, it could have changed dramatically, either upward or downward.

T. Wilson said to me, "We just had to find a way of managing this risk and getting it under control." He said, "I called the guy who was the chief buyer and said, 'Look, for these reasons, we have to find a way of stabilizing the risks in this program, and we think we need to look at some form of hedging policy.'" Well, this was in the 1960s. Today, hedging policies are perfectly normal events. We hedge currencies, we hedge material prices, we hedge oil prices; but at that time it was pretty revolutionary. Anyway, this guy understood the basis of it, went out, and was effectively buying aluminum ahead of rates. The market suddenly turned against [Boeing], they lost a ton of money, and they had to go to the market and announce an exceptional loss.

Managing Your Career

T. Wilson, as the chief executive of the company, had to go to all the big institutional investors in New York and explain what had happened. You start off with the investors, then you go to the analysts, and then eventually—because the analysts talk to the press— you have to talk to the press about it.

Eventually, this guy finished talking to the press. He was having lunch with a journalist, and the first thing this journalist said to him was, "I sure was sorry to hear about the loss on your hedging book on aluminum, but I sure as hell hope you fired the son of a bitch who was responsible for it." There was a bit of a pause, and I said to T. Wilson, "Well, what did you say to him?" He said, "I looked this guy straight in the eye and I said to him, 'You *what?* And learn that lesson all over again? For sure as hell I didn't fire the guy.'"

That's a great story that tells you about how management interacts with the guys that have to do the job. It's also a lesson that tells you, in management terms, that you only have to be right 51 percent of the time to be on the right side of the curve. Here was a guy who had stood up and defended a guy who had cost the shareholders and the company an immense amount of money and kept the guy on in the belief that the guy would never, ever make that mistake again.

That always stuck in my mind, when I've had guys working for me who've made some seriously big mistakes. It's very unusual for a high-quality person—and hopefully when you put guys in these positions they are high-quality people—to make the mistake a second time around. That was another big lesson for me in this business.

TAKEAWAYS

⚔ Everyone makes mistakes, regardless of career experience, length of service or seniority. Firing someone for making a mistake may be an error on your part. Once that person has made a mistake and realized the reasons behind it, they are highly unlikely to ever repeat their actions.

꽥 Trying something new and untested can lead to mistakes, which should be accepted as part of the learning curve and used as a foundation for future projects. You may find you learn best from your failures.

Challenge Ideas, Not People

John Stewart

Former Director, McKinsey & Company

CHALLENGING IDEAS almost always improves the idea, but challenging ideas is often confused with challenging the person who holds the idea. There was one chairman, who came up the finance route, who cared a lot about financial matters and cared a lot about pay.

Managing Your Career

He really tried to figure all kinds of ways to get pay for his managers. He had a hundred managers together for a planning session, and he described how he had a "pay program" that would increase their pay and his pay at a time when people were being laid off and pay was being reduced for a lot of workers. Well, among these hundred managers there were many who believed the executives should be taking the same pay cut as the workers.

One of them stood up and said—I'll use William—"William, we don't like that plan. Some of us don't like that plan. Some of us think that we ought to be taking a pay cut." Whereupon William flew into a tirade, one of the most unusual tirades I've ever seen by a chief executive of a major corporation—a multibillion-dollar corporation—and disbanded the whole meeting.

When that happens, the message goes out: "Whatever you do, don't say anything critical, because the boss can't take it." And so very important things never get to the top, and this loneliness increases, this isolation increases—and it is highly destructive.

There is another chief executive—well known—who yells, screams, shouts, and swears at his people. They were talking about an acquisition, and the chief executive said, "How many people do we have down there looking at that acquisition?" and the answer came back, "We've got thirty people doing due diligence."

The chief executive said, "You've got to be kidding. That's a tiny little company. We'll destroy it while we're doing due diligence. Why are we doing something that stupid?" And there was silence in the room. And this most junior lawyer said, "Well, sir, it's because no one wants you to find something they missed, and so everybody is sending their people down there to find out everything possible. So the reason we're doing it, sir, is you."

And the chief executive said, "Frank"— everyone was waiting, not knowing quite what to expect—"I believe you're right. I believe that's probably exactly what happened. Okay you guys, let's get more reasonable; I promise you I won't kill anyone if you miss some things, but let's stop this madness." And so there was an openness. Now clearly it had not always been that way, or else the vice chairs and the others would have spoken up a little faster.

One of the safest things to do is to say to a chief executive tactfully, "Gee, that's wrong." Not "You're wrong," but "Gee, that's wrong." Because you usually get thanked rather than thrown out of the office. Although sometimes you get thrown out, you rarely get fired. It's usually not career ending, and very often it's career making. So I'd really think hard about how to create an environment as a manager so your people challenge your ideas.

TAKEAWAYS

⊰ You should encourage comments
   and suggestions, and hand them out
   to your coworkers. Ideas are often
   improved by challenging them, but
   you must take care in how the idea is
   challenged.

⊰ There is a distinct difference between
   challenging the idea itself and challenging the person who presented the
   idea. Phrasing a challenge that criti-
   cizes the person rather than focuses on
   the idea creates animosity and leads
   nowhere.

⊰ Managers need to create an atmos-
   phere in which people are free to challenge ideas and in which individuals
   are receptive to feedback.

The Virtuous Circle of Competence and Confidence

Gill Rider

Director General, Leadership and People
Strategy, Cabinet Office UK

Managing Your Career

ONE OF THE THINGS that I learned
very early on in my career was the relationship between confidence and competence.
If you're competent in something, you feel
and exude confidence. And that in itself
feeds the competence, and competence feeds
the confidence—it's a wonderful, virtuous
circle.

I've often found, when I'm helping coach
or counsel people, that it's one of the most
obvious and yet hardest things to see yourself. At one point in my career, I had been
working on a very big client sales initiative
for a long time. We came right up to the
wire and then we lost it. What happened to
me was my confidence just plummeted at
that point.

As time went on, I realized that [my loss
of confidence] was very much affecting the
way people looked at me, and the questions
they were asking were all about my competence. I realized that, actually, while my
competence was as good as it had ever been,
because my confidence had taken a knock,
they weren't seeing the competence.

Managing Your Career

There was a downward spiral, which ultimately led to an enormous level of stress, because if you don't exude confidence, people don't see that you're competent, and the competence isn't there to build the confidence—and down you go. I really had to pull myself together and say, "Well, look, your competence is as good as ever; just work to get your confidence back up."

I've often found this is particularly true when I'm counseling women; they come in, and they're very competent individuals and really can't understand why they're not either getting the most challenging opportunities, or they're not getting considered for promotion.

It very often comes across in terms of the level of confidence that they are exuding to the decision makers. I find, particularly with women, that they get themselves into a mode of believing that we live in a meritocracy, and the meritocracy ought to just see that they're doing a competent job. So I spent a lot of time explaining the confidence/competence cycle, just talking to women about how being competent is not enough—you have to show people how confident you are.

One of the reasons that this is always very sensitive with women is that they don't want to appear to be egocentric or arrogant. They think that by showing and demonstrating confidence, they're taking too much of the merit onto themselves, rather than the team that's doing the work. So it's always very important to talk about the different balances between confidence and being assertive about your views rather than arrogant and self-centered about them.

I really do think that in most situations where you find somebody is not performing, it's quite often because their confidence is down. You have to help them build the competence to get the confidence up, and it is a virtuous circle.

TAKEAWAYS

⚟ If you're competent in something, your confidence will rise accordingly. There are different levels of confidence, such as being assertive about your views, that can be positive attributes in the business world.

⚟ In order to develop your own career, you should consider how other people view you. If you come across as lacking in confidence, people often automatically assume you are lacking in competence.

⚟ If you fail in a task, try not to let it overshadow your competence and ultimately your confidence in future projects. Everyone makes mistakes at some point.

Take Ownership of Your Own Development

Jay Conger

*Henry Kravis Research Chair Professor
of Leadership at the Kravis Leadership Institute,
Claremont McKenna College*

Managing Your Career

EVERY MANAGER and executive basically owns his or her own development as a leader. Let me illustrate with this story, which captures the fact that you and I have to be masters of how we develop as leaders.

The story is set many, many years ago when I was a little boy, actually four years old, and my parents took myself, my older brother, and little sister to southern France. On a very beautiful day, my mother took us all down to the hotel swimming pool. What we hadn't known was that she'd gone out and hired the lifeguard to come and teach my older brother how to swim.

We arrived at this very enormous-looking pool—certainly through the eyes of a four-year-old—and out of the corner of my eye, I captured the image of a young Frenchman walking in our direction—lifeguard kind of character—and he headed over directly to us. He must have known that my mother had selected the oldest of the three kids, because he walked right up to my brother, gave him an enormous smile. He said, "Bonjour, mon petit ami." And with that,

he scooped my brother up in his muscular
arms, a bit like a piece of Styrofoam, and
walked him down to the deepest end of the
pool, where the high board was.

Now remember, I'm the second son, and
I actually thought this looked pretty good.
Well, it was a great idea. The man plunks
my brother down on the side, right at the
edge of the water. The lifeguard then turns
over to a pile of little rings, and you'll remember as a child, you have to put little
life rings around children to support them
in the water. He pulls one of these rings out
and he pops open the air-stopper, and
he begins to pat all the air out of the ring.
From my eyes as the competitor, the
younger brother, this is looking very, very
interesting.

With that, the man slides the empty ring
around my brother's waist. He gives him
another smile, this one a little more devil-
ish, and he says, "Bonne chance, mon ami,"
and he throws him into the very deepest end
of the pool. Well, as you might imagine, my
brother immediately goes under; there's

nothing to hold him up. And I'm sitting there again, with kind of a hidden grin, as my brother goes under the water.

Then I looked back. My little sister and mother are just in a panic, but they're like deer in a headlight; they're just not sure what to do. Meanwhile, the lifeguard is simply standing by, watching. My brother goes under, as I mentioned, and then he pops up, gasping for air and flailing. The next thing I know, he heads back under. At this point, even I'm getting in a panic; I'm thinking, "Oh my gosh, this guy's going to actually kill my brother. This is pretty bad!"

Well, my brother pops up again, and this time, he's actually able to stay up. He's figured out a fundamental swimming stroke called the doggy paddle, and he's paddling furiously, and he's able actually to keep himself up for the rest of the lesson.

Now, let me argue that that lesson is how organizations will develop their talent to be leaders. Let me also point out that it's in many ways a flawed way of development. But let's go back to the beginning of the story.

Managing Your Career

What organizations say is that you're good,
you're talented, and the way they are going
to develop you is by throwing you into jobs
that are over your head, because that seems
to be the best way to develop people. The
lifeguard in this story is your boss.

Now, you notice the boss does not go into
the pool with you; and many bosses are actually busy, so they may actually head off to another swimming pool while you're flailing
around in your pool. But the boss says to
him- or herself, "You know, I've been in
that water before; I figured out how to do it;
I'm sure you will." They also put a little ring
around you. What's that? Well, that may be
HR policies or a training program or the
boss saying, "You know I'm here whenever
you need a little help." But basically, it's il-
lusionary; the support's not there.

Now, the idea is that you'll figure out
how to swim on your own. And if you
don't—well, the idea is that you just weren't
up to this task—sadly, they'll probably move
you back to a smaller pool, maybe even a
kiddie pool, and maybe even take you out of

swimming for good. The moral of the story is that you own your own development, that organizations have a fairly primitive view of how they develop talent. And it's a shame; because ultimately the boss should help you, should be more direct—that life ring should be full of air, and we should move you more gradually into the deep end of the pool.

The lesson is that you, yourself, have to take initiative in order to develop yourself as a leader. You have to proactively seek out coaching and guidance. At times, it'll be awkward, because you'll feel you're revealing your own weaknesses. You may have certain bosses who may not be open to people seeking out coaching and feedback, but find those opportunities wherever you can. You yourself may have to propose taking courses, seeking experiences, getting a personal coach; but in many ways, you own your development.

In the best organizations, they take it a step further. They actually reward bosses for stepping in and guiding and providing coaches; they actually teach bosses how to coach people; they actually reward bosses for people development. They think much more cautiously and deeply about jobs; and the right jobs, given who you are and what you need in this moment, versus, "Well, let's just throw them in, see how they do." They're also very clever about how you transition into a job, and as you get to more senior levels, they provide support and feedback along the way, as you learn the skills you need in the transition.

TAKEAWAYS

🖺 Most organizations throw talented people in over their heads, figuring they will learn to develop on their own, rather than moving them gradually into areas of greater responsibility. If you find yourself in this situation, speak up.

⚔ Managers and executives should be proactive in seeking help to grow as leaders. You should seek out mentors, courses, and experiences that will help you develop your leadership abilities.

⚔ The best organizations reward bosses for developing leaders—but these organizations are rare. You must take responsibility for your own development.

Never Lose Integrity

Blythe McGarvie

President and Founder,
Leadership for International Finance

THE MOST IMPORTANT LESSON I've learned is, you have to keep your integrity. That's the one thing you can't lose. Your reputation will precede you no matter what you do, and keeping your integrity is the most important thing.

People often say, "What do you mean by 'integrity'? That's such an overused word.

Sure, that sounds like 'mom' or 'apple pie'—
of course you need to keep your integrity."
Well, I call it your values in your innermost
core, and I'll give you an example.

When I first became the chief financial
officer at Bic, the pen company based in
France, I was only there a week. My dishes
hadn't even crossed the Atlantic Ocean to
come and join me in Paris. And I was there
at work, and the boss—the chairman and
president of the company—said to me, "It's
July. I want you to release earnings in two
weeks before everyone disappears for the
holidays." They had never released earnings in July. They always had done that in
September.

I said, "Let me go back and check and see
where we are on the closing of the books, and
I'll get back to you in about an hour." To my
amazement, I found out we didn't even have
a balance sheet that had balanced for the last
four months. We didn't have the proper
records. I said, "How can I release earnings
without a good balance sheet, because that
obviously affects the P&L?" I went to talk to
the chairman, and I said, "I can't do this."

Managing Your Career

I'm sitting there thinking, I have three options. One, I can be a whistleblower and tell the community, "This major company does not have financial controls or financial statements—you've got to understand this." Or two, I could quit. I could say, "Wait a minute, this is a company that does not have the types of controls or the reputation and integrity that I expect a company this size to have, because it will reflect on my own integrity." Or three, I could try and find a way to solve the problem.

So, I talked to the chairman. I went to our public accounting firm, and talked to the major partner there. I said, "We have a major issue here. We need to get some books cleaned up. We need to get some things closed. We only have four weeks to do it." We agreed not to release earnings in July, so the pressure was off me until September, but we really hurried and worked a lot of long hours to be ready for a September release.

The lesson I learned here is that instead of just doing what your new boss wants you to do, think about it first, because it's going to reflect on you. I've changed jobs in my

career. I've gone to different companies;
and within a company, I've changed jobs. It's
only natural to want to feel that you want
to please your boss. The first thing you want
to do is make your boss look good. You
want to please your boss, make sure that he's
happy with your results, but never do it at the
expense of what you believe is right.

Other people were closing the books.
The prior CFO, who had been fired, was
closing the books. I don't know how he
could have done it for the other few
months, because he was giving out P&L
information that was not correct, but I
couldn't do it. Personally, I wanted to make
sure that I could hold my head up high and
explain to the investors and the shareholders, and the family, because the family was a
major shareholder in Bic, that we had num-
bers that you could trust, that were credible,
and that had been checked and balanced.

I think it's so important. This was my
dream job—living and working in France
with a major consumer company—and I
actually thought about getting back on the

plane and leaving. It would have been a mistake. To find something wrong and then leave is not the answer, because you're just letting the chance to keep on festering until somebody else might have the courage to take the risk to speak up and to stand out.

Integrity is the only thing we have. We're born with it; we learn it. We learn it very early in life. Sometimes we might fail. We experience things that might rekindle that integrity, but you always have to be vigilant, because it's the only thing you have. And if you lose it, it takes a long time—if at all—for you to gain it back.

TAKEAWAYS

⚔ No matter what individuals do, their reputations precede them, so it's vital to always maintain your integrity. Although it's natural to want to solve

problems and please the boss, solu-
tions should never come at the expense
of your reputation.

⚎ Integrity means different things to
different people, but it always comes
down to a person's core values. When
you are faced with problems that could
jeopardize your integrity, it's important to look at all the options.

⚎ Once an individual's reputation has
been tarnished or lost, it can be nearly
impossible to regain it. You must
strive to value and maintain your own
integrity.

Three Essential Attributes for Career Advancement

Dina Dublon

Former Chief Financial Officer,
JPMorgan Chase & Co.

As I reflect upon my career and try to articulate what were the three most important behaviors in growing up, in advancing professionally, I would come back to, number

one, being demanding—being demanding
of myself, of my boss, and of the company I
work for. Second, resilience and perseverance, the combination of the two; the ability, once knocked down, to get up and be
focused on the final outcome. And then,
finally, in attitude—a can-do attitude—and
confidence to execute.

Being demanding of myself has meant
focusing on the quality, on the speed, on
the clarity of whatever I was tasked to do.
However, what became very clear early on is
that I needed to be equally demanding of
my boss and of the company.

I joined the bank as a trainee in the
trading floor, and about five months into
joining the bank, I was functioning as a full-
fledged trader. But I realized at that point
that I was on this preset track to remain a
trainee for a full year, and it took initiating
conversations with my boss at that point—
and having quite a few of those conversations—to establish the fact that I was actually
functioning differently, that staying on
that same preset track was not appropriate
any more.

Managing Your Career

From my own perspective it has been: if you don't ask, you don't get. You need to be prepared not to get whatever it is when you ask for it, but unless you ask, there is much less chance of the person knowing what is important to you. Discussing your expectations, your aspirations, with the person you work for is a very good discipline. It's a good discipline for you, and it's actually a good discipline as a manager to be discussing the expectations you have of people working for you.

Moving from that into resilience and perseverance, I have had many examples throughout my career of feeling put down, whether it's in a meeting where I had been told by a manager that my opinion didn't matter, or whether it is being called into somebody's office to be told that I had raised issues in a meeting that questioned the way he was pursuing the business. All those were very upsetting incidents. And the ability, in a way, to go back home and cry but get up the next morning and realize that there is a shining sun and that you can go back and go for what was important to get achieved is something that I think has been extremely important in my own career.

The third point I wanted to make is about confidence and a can-do attitude. This is about more than just confidence; it's about making sure that you *appear* confident, even in those situations where there is a level of anxiety associated with taking on a new role. And the example of having this attitude of "things can get accomplished" is not about not understanding what the obstacles are; it's about realizing there are obstacles to getting things accomplished in a large organization but figuring out how to overcome them as opposed to saying, "Oh, here is a wall I cannot climb over."

When I reflect back on the combination of these three qualities—being demanding of yourself and of the company, resilience and perseverance, and a can-do attitude— those were a very important element in my ability to rise through the organization.

TAKEAWAYS

⚏ Effective leaders often exhibit high expectations, strong resilience and perseverance, and an affirmative attitude. These are the very attributes you'll need to develop in order to rise through your organization.

⚏ You shouldn't hesitate to foster open lines of communications with superiors. They might surprise you with their willingness to assist.

⚏ You must try not to get discouraged by adversity; everyone struggles through difficult times. Try to remain confident no matter what the challenge— and remember it too shall pass.

Make Time for the Unexpected

Lynda Gratton

Professor of Management Practice,
London Business School

THINKING BACK, some of my best ideas have come from the most unexpected places. I have a friend who's a professor at the Royal College of Art, and about three years ago, she said to me, "Lynda, why don't you come and hang around the Royal College of Art with me?" And I said, "Okay."

Managing Your Career

At that stage I was the dean of the MBA Program at London Business School, so my job was to think about the education of the many hundreds of MBA students who come through London Business School. And we teach them in the way that most business schools do—you know, large classes, professor sitting at the front talking, and then maybe some group work.

But hanging around the Royal College of Art, what I was really fascinated by was the way that fine artists are taught. What I saw—and I saw her teaching her artists—is that they work in much smaller groups, often with just one tutor. The thing that was very striking is that each artist is taught how to critique the work of another. That was a real insight for me, and that was an idea that I brought back to my own design of the MBA program at London Business School.

One of the lessons I learned from that is that—you know, it was sort of an odd thing for me to spend time at the Royal College because it wasn't really part of my job description—but sometimes the most interesting ideas that I've had have come from unexpected places. Who would think that the Royal College would help me think about London Business School?

What I learned was that if you spend all your time with people who are just like you, you just hear the same thing over and over again. If you want to hear new things, you'd better spend time with people who are very different from you. Over the years I've thought about how I might do that, and I think one thing is that it's quite difficult actually to move outside of your boundaries, but it's really important. I think it's really important to spend time with people who are different from you—different things, different personalities, different countries, different types of organizations. But to do that, you have to give yourself time in your life for serendipity to enter. You actually have to open yourself up to the possibility of the unexpected coming into your life. And one of the ways I think you have to do that is to give yourself space.

Managing Your Career

If you fill your diary up every single moment of the day, then all that happens in your life is you do the expected. It's only when you give yourself time that the unexpected can come in, and serendipity can happen.

TAKEAWAYS

⛥ You should look for ideas in unexpected places. It can be very difficult to move outside comfort zones and boundaries, but it is extremely important to do so.

⛥ You should intentionally spend time with people who are different from you. You should mix with people who have different personalities and different interests, and who come

from different organizations and
countries.

✠ When you open yourself up to the
possibility of the unexpected, you give
yourself space to experience new things
and new people. You might even be
stimulated to come up with your best
ideas.

Always Be Resilient

Peter Ellwood

Chairman, ICI

A KEY LESSON for any manager is to be resilient and tenacious. In a way, any business manager is a bit like a boxer: they will always get knocked to the canvas. But the strength of a really good boxer is that they will get up again because they feel so determined to win. Equally, a businessman will receive setbacks and disappointments, but

the good ones will always get off the canvas
and get back up because they feel passionately about what they want to do.

An example of that for me was when I was
at TSB, and we knew we had a lot more people on the payroll than necessary—in fact,
it seemed to me that we needed about five
thousand fewer people—and we'd arrived at
that after a lot of analysis. I then had to
speak to the old management and say, "Hey,
we have to take out five thousand people
from a payroll of about twenty-five thousand." Their initial reaction was, "Well, this
is completely wrong. Not only do we not
have to take anybody out, we should actually
be putting more people in." So I then had
to demonstrate to them that their level of
productivity for profit, sales, turnover—
everything—was much lower than that of the
competition.

They rationalized this and said, "Yes, but
you can't look at it like this, we have a different image," and so on and so forth. They
said, "It can't be done. If you do it, you will
get no support from anybody. And if you

push it, all the unions will go; they'll take the people on strike, and it simply can't happen." I'd only been with the company a few months at this time, and they said, "Why don't you go back and do some macrostrategic thinking, and we'll manage the business on a day-to-day basis? You needn't worry about it; we've got it all under control."

This made me very angry, and I said, "Absolutely no way. We're going to do it; it's just a question of how we do it." In the end, I had to fire a lot of those senior managers to push this through with some new, more vibrant and energetic managers who understood that if we didn't do this, nobody would have a job because there wouldn't be a company.

That was not a particularly easy thing to do. You can only do it because of the great pushback you get; you can only do it by being tenacious and resilient, and keeping going time after time after time.

You must then be very, very resilient and massively tenacious about pushing [the change] through, because the only thing you

can be sure about is that the people who
have created a problem will not turn round
and say, "Oh gosh yes, I remember now,
I've created this terrible problem; I'm aw-
fully sorry, I will help put it right." What
they will do is to defend and rationalize failure, and they will not accept that they have
to change. As somebody coming in fresh to
a company, you have to force [the change]
through; and do not expect it to be easy, because it won't be.

Resilience is like life; it never stops. It
goes on and on and on. You must always be
resilient. You must always expect, whatever
you are doing, to get knocked to the canvas
from time to time. And you can't say, "Well,
I've reached this particular position in my
career, therefore I am immune to being
knocked to the canvas," because nobody is
immune to that. So you need to be resilient
and tenacious throughout your career. You
will be knocked to the canvas and you will be
attacked, whether it's by shareholders, staff,
or the press. You will be knocked down. The

beauty of the great manager is to get up again, because you believe passionately in what you are doing.

TAKEAWAYS

⫍ A good business manager has the spirit and resilience of a boxer; you may receive setbacks and disappointments but you will get back up off the mat because you feel passionately about what you want to do.

⫍ People hostile to change will defend and rationalize failure. If you are coming in fresh to a company, you must be prepared to force change. If you need to push an unpopular initiative through, be prepared to use a velvet glove.

Managing Your Career

⚔ If you experience a failure, arrange a
   meeting with your supervisor; lay out
   where you think you went wrong, what
   you've subsequently learned, and what
   you would do differently next time.

Nothing Succeeds Like Success

Jeffrey Pfeffer

Thomas D. Dee II Professor of Organizational Behavior at the Graduate School of Business, Stanford University

ONE OF THE INTERESTING things I've learned in my own life is that people love success, and that success causes individuals to reconstruct, rethink, and rerememember things that aren't true. I still recall a

meeting at the American Sociological Asso-
ciation a long time ago, and my dear friend
Paul Hirsch—who was at that time teaching
at the University of Chicago—and I were sitting at a bar and having a drink. And he said
to me, "Jeffrey, we're pretty good friends.
I'd love to ask you a question." I said, "Of
course, Paul, anything you want to know."

He said, "Well, my colleagues at the University of Chicago were talking the other day
about what a shame it was that you had not
joined the University of Chicago and that
you'd gone to the University of Illinois"—
which was my first job, and by then I had
moved on to the University of California
at Berkeley. He said, "My colleagues were
wondering why you had chosen Illinois over
Chicago." I said, "Paul, your colleagues
shouldn't wonder about that at all. The
University of Chicago rejected me." He
said, "You're kidding! My colleagues re-
membered having made you an offer!"

I think that is, of course, a very interesting
principle that you see in lots of aspects of life.
If you ask people how they voted in a presi-

dential election, it turns out that way more than the percentage who actually voted for the winner remember having voted for the winner. We like to associate, I think, with things, people, and causes that are successful.

The obvious example, and it's so obvious that it's almost trite, is Enron. When Enron was apparently successful, and the word "apparent" is obvious, because if you read the book *The Smartest Guys in the Room*, you will see that Enron began its accounting fraud from the very beginning of 1985. This wasn't something recent, and the evidence suggests that Enron probably never was profitable.

But when Enron was the darling of the stock market, it was also on *Fortune*'s list of most admired companies, and its executives were very much lauded in the business press, which tells you about following, of course, the business press. So success, I think, forgave a lot of things.

Success forgives a lot of things. Jack Welch and General Electric are quite successful, so people don't remember the fact that General Electric has been accused of, and actually successfully prosecuted for, all kinds of environmental pollution, including rivers in New York. Then, General Electric was accused and successfully prosecuted for antitrust violations in the industrial diamond business. General Electric has laid off hundreds of thousands of people. But because of the aura of success, all of this is forgotten. So I think, in that sense, success brings plaudits and brings selective perception and selective memory.

By the same token, once Enron was exposed, then everybody piles on, and everybody says, "Oh, we knew it all along. We always told you so." And everybody comes out of the woodwork and piles on. So, I think, you can see both sides of that in the same story.

The lesson here is really an interesting one. One of the things I find when I teach my students an elective course called "The Paths to Power" is that the students are always concerned about how their behavior is going to affect other people, and whether people are going to remember ten or fifteen years later what they have done and whether or not they said something that offended someone.

What I keep telling them is that, if they are successful, people will be happy to be associated with them, and people will forgive them many mistakes and many impolitenesses, simply because people want to be associated with winners and disassociated from losers.

The lesson here is that success brings its own rewards, and to the extent you are successful, you can get away with a lot.

TAKEAWAYS

⧤ Individuals have a need to associate themselves with success, even at the expense of accurate memory. This need might cause you to reconstruct events

that you experienced or make up
events that never transpired.

⊣⊦ People will forgive or forget previous
transgressions of people and companies currently achieving success. You
must ask yourself "is it okay to behave
unethically or participate in negative
practices in order to accomplish a
goal, knowing that success will forgive
indiscretions?"

⊣⊦ Individuals will jump on the band-
wagon and disassociate themselves
from failures and wrongdoings. You
should realize that perceptions or mis-
perceptions about an organization will
affect its bottom line.

A Designed Life

Richard Pascale

*Writer, consultant, and Associate Fellow,
Saïd Business School, Oxford University*

AN IMPORTANT LESSON for me of a
personal nature was this notion of an in-
vented life, of a designed life. And it arose
for me in the second year of getting my
MBA. Having invested the time and all the
money it takes to pay tuition at Harvard,
I found myself in my second year going
through the motions of recruiting for real
companies and being very uneasy about how

Managing Your Career

I could possibly survive working in a real job with—and I know it sounds very self-indulgent—so little holiday built into the design of work, at least in the United States in the 1960s, which was at most two weeks a year, if you were lucky.

One day in this fabulous course on strategy, I found myself drifting out of the topic at hand and thinking for the first time in my life, owing to the fact that the professor teaching this course was absolutely a phenomenal guy, that maybe I'd like to teach, which was a truly novel idea. And I thought a bit about that and I said, "If you're going to teach, you probably have to do a little consulting because if you're not trying it out and testing it out in real organizations, you could really end up in the ivory tower somewhere, and for business that might be fatal."

So, I contemplated that a few more, whatever it was, minutes of daydreaming. And then I thought, "Yes—and I hate to say it—but you've got to write it down because if you don't put it on paper you don't really see how full of shit you are, because it's on paper that you see the holes in your argu-

ment and the failures to the logic." And
then I thought a bit further and I said,
"What about this? What if I could have a life
where I could teach a quarter of the year,
consult a quarter of the year, write a quarter
of the year, and have a holiday for a quarter
of the year?" I was thinking that would be
seriously cool. I almost levitated off my seat
with excitement at this wild and crazy
thought. And then, of course, reality got a
grip on me, and I went back to focusing on
the class and treated this initially as something that was clearly impossible. But I
couldn't let go of the idea.

In fact, when you teach at a school like
Stanford Business School, where I spent
twenty years, and it's based on a quarterly
system, and if you're crazy, you can actually
do all your teaching in one quarter. You
have to be seriously crazy, but it's possible.
That gives you two quarters, one during
which you can do some consulting and another in which you do your writing, and that
gives you your summer.

So it turned out that, in fact, I could put
together a life where those pieces were in

place. And I find it really has been the design of my life, and one that is—again, not nearly as self-indulgent as it probably sounds—very regenerative because each of those pieces informs the other. And the holiday part, which might seem, again, over the top, in fact includes opportunities to just get into a very quiet place and do a lot of reading outside my normal line of work or go to remote cultures that see the world through a very different lens than the one I'm embedded in. These are very powerful, upending opportunities to see the world differently and bring a curiosity back to my work.

I think it was Thoreau who said, "Men lead lives of quiet desperation." And I think this particularly arises around work where, somehow, we wall in our imagination when it comes to the high-stakes poker of our career and our jobs and our income. And I think the insight for me, again—quite by accident or perhaps by pain and necessity—was just allowing myself a playful thought about what might be possible well outside of the boundaries of what one was expected to do with an MBA from Harvard Business School.

Managing Your Career

I think the trick in all of this is, try to approach something as vital as work with the same spirit that we approach our hobbies. If it was something you could play at, like you do the things you do for fun, what would it look like? Allow yourself, at least, to consider that possibility. And finally, I guess, stealing from Stephen Covey, begin with the end in mind, with that kind of crazy idea, something that seems out of reality but is somehow calling to you, as the end point where you're going to end up. How do you begin now with what you have and start to put the pieces together to design that life, to invent the life that really works for you?

TAKEAWAYS

◁ Many individuals are averse to risk or chance with their career paths and settle for the standard journey. You

should keep your minds open when
you weigh career opportunities.

- ⚏ You should approach a career like you
might approach a hobby: with enthu-
siasm, creativity, and optimism. You'll
experience more career satisfaction
this way, and you'll discover your pas-
sions, talents, and convictions.

- ⚏ Successful leaders envision where
they want to go, and map out the process for getting there. You should do
the same. By putting your ideas on
paper, you might encourage your own
accountability.

Learn When to Follow Your Instincts

Sir Michael Rake

Chairman, KPMG International

I THINK ONE THING that is very important about leadership is to learn when to follow your instincts. I think you can end up in too much analysis—too much review, endless data—trying to get to an objective and factual conclusion on every issue you face. Sometimes you just need to follow your instincts, because often they can be absolutely right.

Sometimes my experience has been that, on occasions when I've not followed my instincts—when I've felt really strongly about something and I've delayed—it's been costly. This can mean instinct around a strategic issue; where you face something that arises because of a change in legislation or regulation or publicity, or you feel there's something you need to do. If you're not careful, an organization will tend to analyze [an issue] to death because people don't want to make decisions.

People are frightened of things that change direction, and I think that was particularly the case for us recently, when we had in accounting the kinds of issues around corporate governance scandals in the United States, around what auditors and accounting firms do. I think, following Sarbanes-Oxley, we did realize that we'd had an ambition to establish a global legal capability. As soon as we started to see what was developing around the regulators' reaction to these scandals, it struck me very, very rapidly that we weren't going to be able to continue with our ambitions in legal services.

It was a distraction to our core business, which we really needed to focus on. When we talked to people [our move into legal services] was not seen well"—by politicians, by regulators, by journalists—and it was quite clear to me we needed to make a quick decision. We just needed to say, "This is not going to work. We can analyze this to death, but it isn't going to work." I think by doing that we were able to move very rapidly—we got a lot of credit for [separating from the legal side], we got clarity, we quickly executed it, and we separated it cleanly. I think everyone appreciated that, including the people who were involved—i.e., the people we were separating from. That was an example where following your instincts can really work when those occasions arise.

When you're a leader and you have strong views, or you have strong instincts because you've been there a long time, obviously you need to be able to convince people that you're right about these things. And I think this is quite difficult. Part of it has to be your own self-confidence around the business you're in. Part of it has to do with the way you communicate with your people; that you can explain to them that you've quickly understood the issues. And part of it, of course, is the trust those people have in you, because then, particularly if you emerge as a leader within an organization, it's because people trust you. I think when you see people coming in—and I've seen it many, many times in clients—when you bring in a new chief executive, it's much more difficult. You can see then, if they come too instinctively, too quickly, there isn't a sense of belief in what that individual is trying to do, and that can undermine the process.

So when you come into an organization as a completely new leader, it's much more difficult to jump to those conclusions. You need to have gone through the process of appearing to have listened at least, or really to have listened, to what people tell you. And to demonstrate you understand the business before you make big decisions. Otherwise you simply don't take the people with you—and you need to take the people with you.

The question of when to rely on data and when to rely on instinct is a really difficult issue. Generally, for me at least, what happens is that when I have a strong feeling of the issue I will want to see some data to make sure that prima facie, it supported what I was feeling. Where I'm not quite clear what the answer is, that's the time when one would want to have more data. I think, again, you don't want to overanalyze it, but you do want to talk to people to get a feeling for [the issue].

Many things require an understanding of the emotional element of the people involved, require you to understand the business and the environment you're in. Your antennae need to tell you, "What environment am I in? What is the reaction of the marketplace? What is the reaction, in our case, of the regulator? What will be the PR implications of this?" This is absolutely as—if not more—important than data.

I've seen cases in our own organization where the overanalysis of data is an excuse for not making a decision, or it's a defensive mechanism to be able to prove to somebody that if your decision was wrong, you'd analyzed the data. Therefore, it was a defense against making the wrong decision. And I don't think that works.

I would say that the single most important lesson to remember is that, to a degree, you have to follow your instincts in order for your business to be successful. Life is not black and white, life is not simple: you have to deal with a number of paradigms and you have to deal with confusion. So in order to deal with the world that's somewhat chaotic and extremely fast moving, you have to have the right antennae and you have to rely on your instincts. Otherwise the battle's lost before you've made the decision.

— ◆◆◆ —

TAKEAWAYS

— ◆◆◆ —

✒ Sometimes you need to follow your instincts because they are often absolutely correct. People are frightened of change; but if you believe strongly in the objective, you must encourage others to follow.

✒ There are three aspects important to "following your instincts": self-confidence; how you communicate with your people and explain that you've quickly understood the issues; and the trust your people have in you.

✒ You should follow your instincts when next asked to make a minor decision and then evaluate the outcome. Later, you can draw upon this experience for future decision making.

The Long-Range View over Short-Term Expediency

Gerry Roche

Senior Chairman, Heidrick & Struggles

THE MOST IMPORTANT perspective to have in life is to have the long-range view over the short-term expediency. That's at the core of our business and every business. It's at the core of your relationships with each other—with your wife, friends, and family—and at the core of your relationship with whatever God you might worship.

Roberto Goizueta, the former chairman and CEO of Coca-Cola, once asked me if I was interested in a search to find a CFO for Coke. My insides were going crazy because I knew that he had a very good guy who was the CFO of Coca-Cola Europe.

I said at that meeting, "Roberto, before you commission this search; do you know your CFO in Europe?" He replied, "I just got this job, so no, I've never met him. I don't even know his name, who is he?" I told him his CFO of Europe was a guy named Doug Ivester.

I got a call two weeks later from Roberto, and he said, "Gerry, I can't thank you enough. I met with this man, he's my answer. Do I owe you a fee?" And I said, "No, not for two weeks' work and not for that. But there'll be a time, Roberto, we would like to do more work for Coke; but God bless you and I'm happy." Doug Ivester turned out to be a first-rate CFO, so much so that he became the president of Coke.

Managing Your Career

Eight years after that, I got a call from Roberto Goizueta. He said, "Hey, Gerry, I am the chairman of the search committee for Kodak. They told me that I should have a beauty contest and take a look at a couple of firms around. But I remember you and your integrity and honesty from ten years ago, and I appreciate the favor you did me with Douglas. If you are willing to do this search, you've got it. Come on down to Atlanta, and we'll talk about it and write up the specs." Bing-bang, no competition, no shoot-out, and we got the search for the chairman and CEO of Kodak.

Eight years is the long-range view. I think everything comes down to the long-range view.

I've just finished Nike within the last six months, where we had what I thought was a great candidate a year ago. We presented him to Phil Knight, the board, and the lead director. Everybody liked him a lot; his personality and his experience were fine. I personally wound up doing the references on this fellow. They weren't bad; they just weren't dead on. I can always sense that—instead of, "Oh, he's tremendous; you'd be lucky to get him, I don't think you'll ever get him." I know how to take references and I know the difference between the pulse of a great one and one that's modulating and waffling. His references were modulating and waffling just enough to give me angst and heartburn.

I was sighing and saying to myself, "Dear God, I've been doing this search for six months, it could be over. But I have to tell Phil what I found out and I have to be honest about my doubts about this person."

I told Phil Knight, and we wound up doing more references on him and flushing him. I said to Nike, "It would have been easy for me to say, 'Hey, he's all right.' But I'm saying, 'Hey, I want to feel Knight's respect twenty years from now. Phil Knight has a great company; he deserves to have a great CEO. He doesn't deserve to have one who has yellow flags.'"

The long-range view over the short-term expediency wins every time—not immediately; sometimes it's painful and it costs. But if you have faith in the future, you have the long-range view.

TAKEAWAYS

⚔ If you're hiring, you should take your time to recruit. You must get the best possible person for the job, even if it takes longer than you'd ideally like.

⚔ You should always question your first choice for the role. Are you taking him or her on because it is the easy option or because he or she is the perfect person for the job? And be honest about your doubts—once a decision has been made it will be difficult to justify your point of view if something goes wrong.

- Doing a colleague or peer a favor can pay dividends in the long term; as people move up the career ladder, they may recall your kindness and call on you for help in the future. A long-term approach can win you respect.

Work as a Learning Experience

Sir George Mathewson

Former Chairman,
The Royal Bank of Scotland Group

Managing Your Career

DON'T WASTE your time worrying about what may happen in the future; just keep building your strengths doing a very good job and educating yourself for the future. Then if your career works out, it will work out.

After university I did a PhD; I don't really know why, except that it seemed like a good idea at the time. I then became part of the brain drain to the United States and worked for five years with Bell Aerospace in the United States doing all sorts of useful things. At one time, I was a world expert on air-to-ground helicopter gunfire—not something that has stood me in particularly good stead since.

I came back to the United Kingdom and went into development capital with 3i, which was then ICFC, and that taught me a lot. Again, I took that job, I came back; I had a PhD and an MBA, and the MBA stood me in much better stead than the PhD when it came to getting a job.

I joined the business—development capital, which I knew nothing about. I took to it

and went very quickly through the ranks at
3i. Then I was headhunted to run the Scot-
tish Development Agency, which was large,
complex, and had political and leadership
dimensions. I learned a lot about management there.

When I did that, people said to me,
"You've got a background in technology and
finance. You must have really thought to put
it all together to do this wider job at the
SDA." I was managing thousands of people,
and I'd never managed more than five people before that. The answer was, of course,
that I hadn't given thought to any of that.

But I'd gone through these jobs and done
all of them pretty well. Young men, in my experience, often spend too much time thinking about their next job rather than focusing
on their current job and doing it well. I find
young women are a bit better at that.

All of these things were educational exer-
cises, and I'd like to think that's never
stopped. People should always look at their
jobs like that; I find too many get put into

pigeonholes, and too many allow themselves to be pigeonholed.

I think you have to continually look to expand your capabilities and not allow yourself to sit still. Throughout all of the things we do, none of us has any clue as to what the future holds. You've just got to make yourself fitter to cope with whatever there is. It's the same philosophy for both people and companies.

TAKEAWAYS

-⧚ By making time to pursue your interests, you broaden the range of future opportunities. This way, you can optimize every opportunity in your current role.

Managing Your Career

🙣 You must treat each job that you are in as a valuable learning experience. Focus on your current job and do that to the best of your abilities; the future will take care of itself.

Paul Anderson is the chairman of Spectra Energy. Mr. Anderson is also a director of Qantas Airways and BHP Billiton.

Mr. Anderson started his career at Ford Motor Company, holding various positions from 1969 to 1972. He was planning manager from 1972 until 1977, and then joined PanEnergy. Over the ensuing years, Mr. Anderson served in various leadership roles within PanEnergy, culminating in becoming its chairman, president, and CEO.

In 1998 Mr. Anderson moved to BHP, where he was managing director and CEO until its merger with Billiton in 2001. He then became managing director and CEO of BHP Billiton until his retirement from the company in 2002.

Mr. Anderson returned to Duke Energy as chairman and CEO in November 2003. He then became chairman of Spectra Energy in 2007 when Duke Energy's natural gas business was spun off into a new company called Spectra Energy.

Jay Conger is the Henry Kravis Research Chair Professor of Leadership at the Kravis Leadership Institute, Claremont McKenna College.

About the Contributors

Prior to his academic career, Professor Conger worked in government and as an international marketing manager for a high-technology company. After moving into academia, he became a research scientist at the Center for Effective Organizations at the University of Southern California. He then became the executive director of its Leadership Institute.

Professor Conger was subsequently invited to join London Business School in 1999 in the role of Professor of Organizational Behavior. He remained there until he took his current position at Claremont McKenna College in 2005.

Dina Dublon is the former CFO of JPMorgan Chase & Co. In this role she was responsible for financial management, acquisitions, corporate treasury, and investor relations. Currently, Ms. Dublon serves on the boards of Accenture, Microsoft, and Pepsi.

In 1981 she joined Chemical Bank's capital markets group as a management trainee on the trading floor. She was integral to the structuring and negotiation of the mergers of Chemical Bank with Manufacturers Hanover, Chase, JPMorgan, and Bank One.

In 1994 Ms. Dublon was named corporate treasurer, and subsequently head of corporate planning and chief financial officer in 1999. She stepped down from her role as chief financial officer at the end of 2004.

About the Contributors

Peter Ellwood is the chairman of Imperial Chemical Industries (ICI), a position he has held since June 2004. He is also a fellow of the Chartered Institute of Bankers and a director for First Data.

Mr. Ellwood began his career at Barclays in 1961 and rose to become chief executive of Barclaycard from 1985 until 1989. During this time he was also a director of the board of Visa European Union. He was chairman of the board of Visa International from 1994 to 1999.

He joined TSB Bank as Chief Executive of Retail Banking in 1989 and became Group Chief Executive in 1992. Following TSB's merger with Lloyds Bank in 1995, Mr. Ellwood became Deputy Group CEO of Lloyds TSB, then Group CEO.

In June 2003, Mr. Ellwood became deputy chairman of ICI, one of the world's largest producers of specialty products and paints. One year later, he became its chairman.

Sir Richard Evans is the chairman of United Utilities, a position he has held since 2001.

Sir Richard started his career at the Ministry of Transport and Civil Aviation. He joined the British Aircraft Corporation (BAC) and was promoted to commercial director of the Warton Division of British Aerospace (BAe) in 1978.

In 1981, he became deputy managing director for BAe Warton. Three years later he was made deputy managing director of the British Aerospace Military Aircraft Division. One year later, he was appointed to the board of British Aerospace as marketing director, and the following year he became chairman of the British Aerospace Defense companies.

He was appointed CEO of British Aerospace in 1990. In 1998 he joined British Aerospace as chairman and continued to chair the company when it became BAE Systems following the merger with Marconi Electronic Systems. In July 2004 he retired from the board but continues to advise the company.

Lynda Gratton currently holds the role of Professor of Management Practice at the London Business School. In this capacity she directs the school's executive program, Human Resource Strategy in Transforming Organizations, which runs in London, the United States, and India.

A trained psychologist, she worked for British Airways for several years as an occupational psychologist, then became Director of HR Strategy at PA Consulting. Professor Gratton also led The Leading Edge Research Consortium, a major research initiative that involved companies such as Hewlett-Packard and Citibank.

Sir George Mathewson is the former chairman of The Royal Bank of Scotland Group, a position he retired from in 2006. He is currently director of NatWest Bank.

Sir George spent the early years of his career in the United States, where, as a professional engineer, he managed research and development programs in avionic systems for Bell Aerospace Corporation.

He joined the board of The Royal Bank of Scotland Group in September 1987 as director of strategic planning and development. In June 1990 he was appointed Deputy Group CEO, later becoming Group CEO in 1992.

An instrumental architect in RBS's acquisition of National Westminster Bank, he was appointed executive deputy chairman in 2000. He became chairman of the RBS Group a year later.

Blythe McGarvie is the president and founder of Leadership for International Finance, a private consulting firm offering a global perspective for clients to achieve profitable growth and providing leadership seminars for corporate and academic groups. In addition, Ms. McGarvie currently serves on the boards of Accenture, Pepsi Bottling Group, St. Paul Travelers, and Wawa.

Ms. McGarvie has operated profitable business units and managed employees in business endeavors from China to France and Finland. Prior to starting Leadership for International Finance, Ms. McGarvie served as executive vice president and CFO for Bic Group.

Richard Pascale is an Associate Fellow of Saïd Business School at Oxford University. He is also the Principal of Pascale & Brown.

Mr. Pascale spent twenty years as a member of the faculty at Stanford's Graduate School of

About the Contributors

Business, where he taught a course on organizational survival.

During his career he has also been a White House Fellow, Special Assistant to the Secretary of Labor, and senior staff on a White House Task Force. Mr. Pascale is an architect of corporate transformation programs and serves as an adviser to top management for a number of *Fortune* 100 companies.

Mr. Pascale is also an accomplished author.

Jeffrey Pfeffer is the Thomas D. Dee II Professor of Organizational Behavior at the Graduate School of Business, Stanford University. Professor Pfeffer has taught at Stanford University since 1979.

Currently, he also serves on the board of directors of Audible Magic and SonoSite. Professor Pfeffer consults to, and provides executive education for, numerous companies, associations, and universities in the United States. He also writes a monthly column on management issues entitled "The Human Factor" for the business magazine *Business 2.0*.

Professor Pfeffer also served on the board of Unicru and has been a visiting professor at the Harvard Business School. He is the author or coauthor of eleven books.

Sir Michael Rake is the chairman of KPMG International. He is also chairman of Business in the Community and on the board of the Prince of Wales' International Business Leaders' Forum.

About the Contributors

Sir Michael joined KPMG (Peat Marwick) in 1972 and worked in Europe, where he ran the audit practice in Belgium and Luxembourg from 1984 to 1986, before moving to the Middle East to run the practice for three years.

After transferring to London in 1989, he became a member of the U.K. board two years later and had a variety of leadership roles before being elected U.K. senior partner in 1998, then international chairman in 2002. He moved on to become chairman of KPMG in Europe and then chairman of KPMG International and senior partner of KPMG in the United Kingdom. During his tenure he has overseen the campaign to ensure that there has been a progressive and pragmatic legislative response post-Enron.

Gill Rider is Director General, Leadership and People Strategy, at the Cabinet Office, UK, a position she was appointed to in February 2006. She also acts as head of profession for HR professionals across government, thereby building up their HR capability.

Ms. Rider started her career in the financial markets, health-care, and government industries. She also worked in the customer service area examining industry best practices. She joined Accenture in 1979 and became a partner in 1990.

With operational responsibility for Accenture's Utilities practice in Europe and South Africa, she also served as chairman of Accenture's United Kingdom and Ireland geographic unit. She then headed the European and Latin American operations of Accenture's Resources operating unit.

Ms. Rider became Accenture's chief leadership officer when the position was created in March 2002. She headed the company's Organization and Leadership Development group, and was responsible for developing the leadership capabilities and professional skills of Accenture's people and fostering a culture that encourages diversity and achievement.

Gerry Roche is the senior chairman of the executive search firm Heidrick & Struggles.

Mr. Roche joined Heidrick & Struggles in 1964 and became senior vice president and eastern manager in 1973. Four years later, he became Executive Vice President, responsible for all domestic operations.

A year later, Mr. Roche became president and CEO. In 1981 he moved into the chairman's role, permitting him more time to conduct high-level international search work. Thirteen years later, Mr. Roche cofounded Heidrick & Struggles's Office of the Chairman with John Thompson.

John Stewart was a director at McKinsey & Company for forty years, specializing in solving problems for technological organizations.

During this time, he worked in several highly technical industries such as aerospace, electronics, and pharmaceuticals. In addition he has worked in several manufacturing industries including automotive, steel, chemicals, and paper.

Mr. Stewart's concentration has been on strategic issues facing these industries, their need to improve operating performance, and the organizational change needed to implement revised strategies or new operational programs. He is now retired.

ACKNOWLEDGMENTS

First and foremost, a heartfelt thanks goes to all of the executives who have shared their hard-earned experience and battle-tested insights for the Lessons Learned series.

Angelia Herrin, at Harvard Business School Publishing, consistently offered unwavering support, good humor, and counsel from the inception of this ambitious project.

Julia Ely, Hollis Heimbouch, and David Goehring provided invaluable editorial direction, perspective, and encouragement. Much appreciation goes to Jennifer Lynn for her research and diligent attention to detail. Many thanks to the entire HBSP team of designers, copy editors, and marketing professionals who helped bring this series to life.

Finally, thanks to our fellow cofounder James MacKinnon and the entire Fifty

Acknowledgments

Lessons team for the tremendous amount of time, effort, and steadfast support they devoted to this project.

—Adam Sodowick
Andy Hasoon
Directors and Cofounders
Fifty Lessons